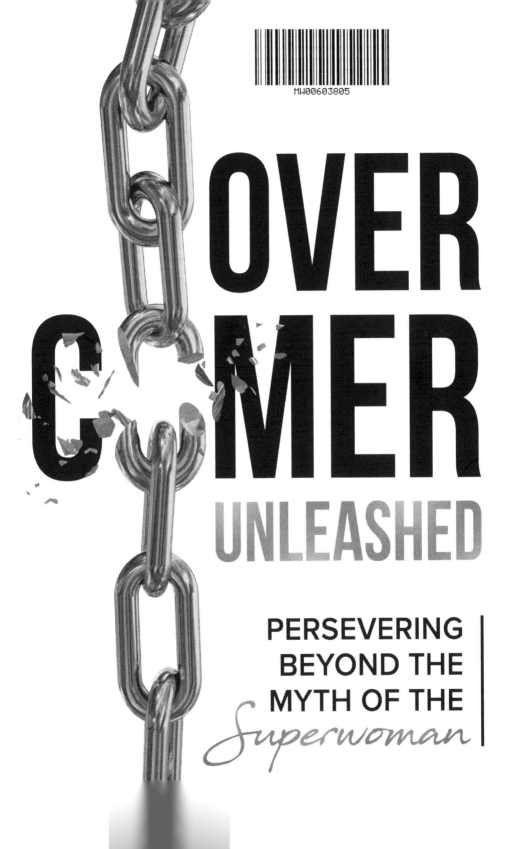

OVER
COMER
UNLEASHED

PERSEVERING
BEYOND THE
MYTH OF THE
Superwoman

OVERCOMER UNLEASHED
Persevering Beyond the Myth of the Superwoman

Frederica Tokponwey
contact@overcomerunleashed.com

ISBN 978-1-943342-31-0
Printed in the USA

Published by: Destined To Publish | Flossmoor, Illinois
www.DestinedToPublish.com

Dedication

The book is dedicated to the courageous women who have
confronted their trauma and taken the challenging path
towards overcoming their worst experiences: I salute you.

LAUREN.
Embrace Your Journey!
IT's Your time
to Shine!

SL

Contents

Contents

Dedication i

Foreword...v

Introduction.. vii

Chapter 1: Sixteen mouths to feed 1

Chapter 2: Sudden death 13

Chapter 3: Wolf in sheep's clothing 20

Chapter 4: Superwoman 28

Chapter 5: Life is a whirlwind.. 35

Chapter 6: Tennessee Lady Vol.. 42

Chapter 7: The Big Apple 54

Chapter 8: Empowered 61

Chapter 9: Love/grief 68

Chapter 10: Savior 76

Chapter 11: Overcomer 85

Foreword

When I was around sixteen or seventeen years old, my mom revealed that she had been a victim of ongoing sexual abuse as a child. I don't remember all of the emotions I felt when my mother disclosed this to me, but one that stands out profoundly is confusion. My mother was by far the strongest woman I knew. I had never seen her cry. She was strong and stiff in her commands, she put business before pleasure, and we never talked about loss. I yearned to show up like her. I cursed myself for crying when I was upset and for falling helplessly in love with my schoolboy crushes. She was a strong Black woman, and my actions proved that I was training to be weak.

Hearing that she had been abused confused me. How could someone have done that to my mother? The woman standing before me could never have been taken advantage of. She was a superwoman with the superpowers of detachment, indifference, nonchalance, and (seemingly) never-ending strength. In the years since that confession, I've learned how the veil of her superpowers was actually her kryptonite.

In these memoirs, my mom will take you through the personal journey that enabled her to stop surviving life and start living. She thought that her putting on an armor of strength would benefit me, but it actually turned out to be a series of defenses that kept each of us hostage individually and caused emotional distance to grow between us.

This book is for every woman looking back at her emotional, mental, and physical wounds who chooses a new reality for herself. This book is for the woman who wants to demolish the facade of being "unbreakable, strong, and emotionless." Let this story grant you permission to be the person trauma didn't give you a chance to be. It's never too late to enjoy the soft life. I'm so proud of your courage, Mom. *Ashia, November* 2023

.

My daughter, Ashia and I

Introduction

The roosters had not begun to crow as I sped down the West Side Highway to work in midtown Manhattan. I arrived in the nick of time, hastened to the locker room, put on my uniform, and headed upstairs to start my workday. As I entered the room, the stillness and readiness of the officers positioned as soldiers provoked me to adopt a severe and militant attitude.

"Attention to roll call." I spoke as the officers opened their memo books.

One of my goals for that day was to remind the officers that even though our assignment was to protect life and property, we had to put ourselves first. We could not be a reliable source of aid if we showed up on the scene with a bag full of emotional, mental, and physical issues. Visually appearing to be fit for duty and mimicking superheroes while possessing the desire to take on the complex tasks of officers did not indicate that we were taking care of ourselves. We often struggled, suppressing the issues plaguing our minds in order to get through the day. We hid any outward expressions of our trauma, appearing unscathed.

In law enforcement, admitting to emotional struggles earns one the "unfit for duty" label. The danger with suppression, however, is that it puts one's issues and emotions in an incubator, where they often grow and multiply, becoming more challenging to bear. By the time the officer retires, the damage has matured into an unmanageable trigger. Revealing our true identities—a mixture of emotions, likes, dislikes, fears, strengths, and weaknesses—is a task. We all want the world to see our best attributes, so we go through life displaying our greatest qualities. We avoid revealing the vulnerable components at all costs because we don't want to be judged based on them.

Insurmountable issues plague the lives of many police officers. They lay hidden under our protective vests, weighing us down emotionally. Financial problems, substance abuse, health issues, domestic violence, mental deficiencies, and job-related stressors show up in our profession when we don't handle them correctly. Unfortunately, the law enforcement culture of always being fit for duty prevents officers from seeking proper help. Loss of employment, being labeled incompetent and unfit, and loss of money due to limited work are some of the reasons officers stay silent.

Working in law enforcement for over twenty-two years placed me in some of life's most demanding situations, including exposure to life-altering tragedies such as 9/11, public scrutiny and criticism, demanding work schedules, racism, cronyism, and sexism. It was a constant fight masking the frustration that sought to impact my heart and mind negatively.

I spent a great deal of my life emotionally hidden. I dealt with a lot of childhood trauma that assisted me in creating a false narrative around my identity and purpose. Sexual abuse, rejection, and the death of my loved ones all left me with different emotional costumes to wear. As a result, the identities of fear, shame, and vulnerability emerged.

I stood before my officers, a strong, seasoned instructor and supervisor who was revered and highly respected, encouraging others to push past their discomfort. But there were times when the cries of my past haunted me. I was able to protect and serve, but I was in constant battle with a wounded teenage girl over my emotional state.

I began my emotional journey with many traumatic experiences but no handbooks on how to overcome them. As a result, my wounded mindset tossed everyone into the penalty box. At the time, I thought my best survival tactic was to continue to show up like a superwoman. Being recognized as one of the nation's top junior track and field athletes gave me a platform on which to be admired, praised, and awarded. What people didn't know about me was that I was suffering silently.

The stop signs of relief on my traumatic road were all hidden. The overwhelming shame, guilt, and emotional pain left me feeling like I had no options. I went through life trying to suppress my traumas without realizing what I had become during the journey—a fraud.

My traumatic experiences produced a superwoman persona within me. A superwoman shows up like she can handle anything or anyone that comes her way. A superwoman knows how to manage life's most difficult challenges without being troubled. A superwoman never shows her weaknesses and always overcomes her troubling circumstances. Even though I appeared to be a superwoman and acted like one, I lacked the aforementioned qualities.

My mother showed up like a superwoman. In my eyes, she handled her problems with ease and never appeared to experience challenges managing life. She petitioned God to help her deal with every circumstance. She believed in God's word, which assured her that all things worked together for good to them that loved God (Romans 8:28).

Born the youngest of sixteen children and raised as a preacher's kid, I was taught to petition and trust God for everything. My father, an anointed preacher of the gospel of Jesus Christ and steadfast prayer warrior, and my mother, an exhorter and encourager who gave her time to serve the less fortunate, gave me a spiritual set of lenses. They served as examples of how to persevere and survive through challenging circumstances. My mother mastered smiling through adversity, and she passed that behavior on to me. Initially, I did not have faith like my parents possessed. I was an immature Christian and often questioned God about the things I experienced. Many times, I felt like I was being punished for not being a good enough Christian. Therefore, instead of telling anyone what I was dealing with, I remained quiet and suffered silently.

Throughout my life, most referred to me as being "superwoman-like." The hard work of showing up and playing the role of excellence allowed me to satisfy the expectations of all despite my secretly enduring a life full of trauma.

In each "part" I played, I continued to show up as a strong Black woman who could aid and protect those within my reach. And while people admired me and acknowledged that I was a force to be reckoned with, I struggled with debilitating time bombs that were chipping away at my soul.

The myth of the superwoman is the furthest from the truth. A superwoman may know how to complete some of life's most difficult challenges, but it often does not come easy. Her hidden qualities include being docile, afraid, and concerned, constantly worried about whether she will complete the task at hand. She cries and wants to be hugged, loved, and considered. A superwoman shows up and does everything effortlessly but always yearns for help. Unfortunately, to protect her vulnerability, she won't ask for it.

When the cameras were off, I dealt with many unseen traumas. I could hide and disguise my pain because I had something working in my favor to distract me from my reality. Even when some of my traumas no longer consumed me, I showed up like a superwoman. I did so for most of my life. It was the only way I could feel comfortable showing myself. It was a way to appear strong, not vulnerable.

Having my vulnerability challenged as a child had motivated me to behave this way. I was encouraged to be a superwoman as a mom because I had a daughter to raise. Desiring to teach her that she had agency over her life pushed me to show up unmoved in front of her. I would later learn that my appearing emotionally and physically stable compromised her ability to deal with her own emotions. She felt like she was "less than" whenever she shared her feelings because she had never seen me be emotionally expressive.

Author Ellen Bass states, "When there has been real harm done by people who should have been trustworthy, there's a deep level of confusion about your own goodness, worth and value."[1]

As I continued to press through, pray, and seek God for help, I became empowered to change. I began seeing my trauma as stairsteps and started a new journey to regain my stolen identity. The power of God helped me triumph over my circumstances. As a result of the trauma I experienced and overcame, I became an example of shame turned inside out, empowering many people to unlock their voices of shame and share their stories. I now operate as a woman with purpose.

Experiences of abuse, neglect, or loss are not the only things that can lead to trauma. Heck! The pandemic-induced isolation that has caused trauma for many of us has often gone unrecognized and impacted various aspects of our lives and mental health.

I encourage you to use this book as an interactive and personal reflection on your own lived experiences. At the end of each chapter, you will find a section of journal prompts called *What's your story?* to encourage you to reflect on your own life as I recount various stories from mine.

Through this process, I hope you begin to find peace, healing, and a clear path towards your own story of "overcoming." You can face your past and know that you do not have to be strong at every turn.

You are not alone.

1

Sixteen Mouths to Feed

"It's a girl."

I popped out, a tall, healthy, chunky baby, ready to take on the world. I was born the sixteenth child to Southerners Jesse and Maria Winley. Yup! You heard that right: I am the youngest of sixteen children—eleven boys and five girls. Everyone had something to say about how many kids my parents had. My mother stated she had not planned to have sixteen children. Her children were a result of God's blessings. You can only imagine the task my parents had raising sixteen kids. But, in my eyes, it was fun. So many of my siblings were old enough to be my parents, so most of my fondest memories growing up involved their kids—my nieces and nephews. I chuckled every time my older nieces and nephews called me "Auntie."

Baby Frederica

Our home was like a mini-NYC Grand Central Station: constant pedestrian traffic in and out of the house, pots and pans on the stove producing spicy smells that elevated one's emotional state. Children ran up and down the stairs tattling on each other, the dogs chased the cats, and Momma was constantly yelling directives.

My daddy was a Pentecostal Bishop in a church in Harlem for over two decades. He was a dynamic preacher of the gospel of Jesus Christ. During his ministry in the late '60s, he would conduct street meetings on the mean streets of Harlem. The rioting, burning, and killing in the ghettos would not keep him from preaching the gospel, even on the streets of the nation's most corrupt city. He was fearless. My father's anointing also allowed him to speak worldwide and preach on many Christian platforms. He was one of the driving influencers of the creation of the Trinity Broadcasting Network (TBN).

Fathering sixteen children came with joys, heartaches, and challenges. My father used his own experiences with his children's issues, such as drug abuse, teenage pregnancy, homosexuality, and interracial marriage, to speak to his congregation. We were often the subject of his sermons. Our deliverance always inspired the church folks. He was a true man of God who empowered, inspired, and motivated people to move beyond their difficult circumstances.

My family

2

Soon, I would realize that I was called to do the same and would help many through their wildernesses.

My father's vision of positively impacting the community involved establishing a drug-addict program and building a Christian school, both in Harlem. He established the Billy Roberts House of Hope, a drug-addict program, by transforming the church basement into a soup kitchen. This program served and fed thousands of people with drug addiction in the Harlem community daily. It accepted and welcomed them every day, whatever their condition. They would pile in, scratching like bugs were invading their bodies and nodding as they waited to eat. The program would feed them, provide them with clothes, inspire them through the preached word, and give them resources to help them transition into a safer, healthier lifestyle. The church was the first place where I saw a person addicted and struggling with drugs. Witnessing their struggle through my own lenses made me feel sorry for them and expanded my perspective.

The Christ Crusader Academy, founded by my father, provided the children in Harlem with a safe Christian environment to learn in. In addition to taking core classes, such as math, science, English, and history, studying and memorizing the word of God was a requisite. As a student of the first graduating class, I gained a spiritual foundation that provided me with the tools to overcome many overwhelming circumstances I endured. In addition, that foundation reinforced my home's values, which entailed petitioning God for all my needs.

My mother and father were Southerners, born and raised in Georgetown, South Carolina. They started their marital journey as teenagers. My mother, affectionately known as "Mariah," was a sweet, gentle soul, born the third child to Alexander and Hattie. Grandpa Alex was a Cherokee Indian. My momma walked this earth displaying her Cherokee heritage on her solid frame, which stood five feet, ten inches tall. Her inheritance allowed her to show her beauty and strength simultaneously.

This superwoman gave birth to sixteen children and nurtured each of us like an only child. She dedicated her life to raising her children and co-labored and served with my father in the ministry domestically and abroad. Many saw her as their own mother, as she opened her heart and home to those in need. When we ate, they ate. What we received, they received. Even though our house was like a bustling hotel, it was a house of hope. It did not matter whether one was a teenage mom, drug addict, senior in distress, victim of domestic violence, or young woman trying to find her way. Momma would take time to nurture and support people and empower them to see new possibilities for themselves. She was an encourager and a woman who gave her time to serve the less fortunate. She always had a smile on her face despite the challenging circumstances she endured. I inherited this trait.

Mom and Dad

4

Being born to Pentecostal parents meant that we lived under some strict guidelines. First, having a father as a pastor meant we stayed in the church. Attending all-night Friday prayer and being in church all day on Sundays for three services was our weekly routine. In addition to church, we would have family prayer on the weekends. We would have to get up at 6 am and give thanks for what God had done for us. The early morning hours made testifying a task for me. After partying all night, my brothers would make it just in time for prayer. With the house packed to capacity and everyone giving their testimony, it always felt like a mini church service.

My father's ministry kept him on the road a lot. He often traveled worldwide, so I cherished any time he spent with me. Going to the beach was something he loved to do in his spare time. Sometimes he would let my siblings, nieces, nephews, and I tag along with him. In the dreadful hours of the morning, "Who wants to come with me to the beach?" would echo throughout the house.

Like little soldiers, we would pop out of bed, still sleepy, rubbing our eyes to restore our vision, and head to the beach with my dad. At the beach, he would talk to God as the birds flew low, just above the water, and the waves softly kissed the shore. Then, like a musical conductor, he would speak out loud, making gestures as he walked along the water as if God were standing next to him. My euphoric moments came from running up and down alongside the edge where the sand and waves greeted one another. It was celestial.

My fondest memories of my father involve our many racing challenges. For an older guy, my father was a fast runner. In front of my house was a small oval island in the center of the street; it was about seventy-five yards long. That was where the competitions between my father and I would take place:

1. He would set the scene of a big track event with many spectators.

2. We would walk to the starting line, which was at the beginning of the island, to begin what I imagined to be our big championship race.

3. He would start stretching his arms and legs in preparation for the race, and I would do the same.

4. He would stay at the starting line and give me a ten-yard lead.

5. Then he would call the race: "Runners, take your mark, get set, go."

We would both start running, trying to beat each other to the finish line. I would run, huffing, and pumping my arms to prevent my father from catching up with me. As we approached the finish line, I could hear him gaining on me, and just before the race ended, he would inevitably catch up with me and win the race. Even though I never won, those were among the happiest moments in my life with my dad. He would always tell me, "You are a fast runner." Those interactions with my dad left me feeling accomplished and empowered. In addition, the races helped shape my competitive drive where sports were concerned.

While growing up, I was highly athletic. Pick-up basketball games, racing, and handball with my brothers, friends, nieces, and nephews were the norm. It was not unusual for there to be a group of neighborhood kids in my backyard. There was always some competitive game taking place. When my brothers played basketball with their friends, it was like watching an actual NBA game. They would dunk, fight, and talk junk like the players in the NBA. I made similar moves back then; I played basketball like the basketball legend, Magic Johnson. I would dribble the ball between my legs and look in one direction but throw the ball in another direction to my teammates. I was a tomboy.

Future gymnast

After getting my share of bumps and bruises from the concrete playgrounds in my neighborhood, I began taking acrobatic classes at the local dance school. I would run there every Saturday in my little blue bodysuit to perfect my skills and prepare for the end-of-year recital. I enjoyed acrobatics so much that I decided I wanted to be a gymnast, but after a year of gymnastics, boredom set in, and I began to grow fond of another sport: track and field.

Fortunately, for me, the gym teacher at my school was a Jamaican track runner. She exposed me to track and field when she took my gym class on a field trip to the Armory. The Armory was located on 135th Street in Harlem and built for the 369th Infantry Regiment, known as the Harlem Hellfighters. The Hellfighters were the first Black regiment to fight in World War I. In addition, the massive building served as a place where many track teams practiced. As a result, some of the nation's top athletes practiced in the Armory.

Empire State Games Champion

It was an exciting trip. We watched all the boys and girls running, jumping, and hurdling. However, as we continued to walk around the Armory, I witnessed some girls crying and vomiting after their races and coaches yelling at their athletes if they were not running fast enough. "Geesh!" I whispered. It looked intense.

We finally got to the coach my gym teacher knew from the track circuit. A short, stout, Black man greeted us. He was the coach of an all-girls track team. When he asked if we wanted to practice with his girls, I yelled, "Yes!" with excitement because I knew I was a fast runner. That day, I ran faster than all the girls I raced with. The adrenaline that I experienced winning race after race was so thrilling that I decided I wanted to run track. My races with Dad had paid off.

The big day came when I finally ran my first organized track meet. My father escorted me, giving me tips along the way. Finally, I arrived at the track meet, ready to compete in my jeans and T-shirt. Everyone else had cool matching uniforms with their team names written across their chests. I was nervous but excited at the same time. We met with my coach, and the adults greeted each other with a handshake. My coach entered me in the 400-meter race, one full lap around the track. I made up my mind that I would be the first to complete this one-lap race. Being an inexperienced runner, I took off like I was running a 100-yard dash when the referee shot the starter pistol. I quickly found out that the race was not only about speed but also about stamina. Even though I was tired and felt like my chest was about to burst open, the competitive drive that dwelled inside me kept pushing me around that track. My winning and running the time I ran had everyone wondering who I was and what team I ran for. My coach was ecstatic and knew that he had a talented girl that he could develop into a great athlete.

For the rest of the school year, I continued going to the Armory from time to time to practice with the track team. Finally, after much convincing, my mother signed me up for the track club at the end of the school year, and I began my career as a track and field athlete. As time passed, I began running, hurdling, and jumping exceptionally well. Then I began competing in track meets all over the country. One of my favorite track meets to run was the Colgate Women's Games in Brooklyn, New York. The Games provide athletic competition that helps the participating young girls and women develop a strong sense of personal achievement and self-esteem while instilling the importance of education in them.

Track granted me exposure to many opportunities that I would not have experienced if I had not been an athlete. Traveling to different states was indeed an experience. Showing up like my father told me I could was empowering. He always knew I was talented enough to compete and do well as a runner among the best. My future was looking bright; I did not know that it would slowly start to dim.

What's your story?

Born the youngest of sixteen children and raised as a preacher's kid, I was taught to petition and trust God for everything. My father, an anointed preacher of the gospel of Jesus Christ, and my mother, a steadfast prayer warrior and encourager who served the less fortunate, gave me a spiritual set of lenses. They served as examples of how to persevere and survive through challenging circumstances. My mother mastered smiling through adversity, and she passed that behavior on to me.

1. What traits, if any, did you pick up from your parents? Do you feel they benefited or harmed you?

_____

_____

_____

_____

_____

_____

_____

_____

2. What was it like growing up? Were there things that made you feel safe or otherwise?

_____

_____

_____

_____

_____

_____

_____

_____

_____

_____

_____

_____

_____

_____

2

Sudden death

The sun had not yet begun showing off when my mother's soprano scream awakened me. I quickly jumped out of my sleep, trying to figure out if I was dreaming. My sister, Charlene, my niece, Jocy, and I ran out of our rooms like soldiers summoned to duty. Clearing the sticky substance from our eyes, we burst through my parents' bedroom door. As my eyes welled up, I stood paralyzed, watching my momma, whom I envisioned as a strong woman of resilience, strength, and power, wailing like a hungry baby.

My father was dead.

Four days before, on Father's Day, my dad had been admitted to the hospital for a routine procedure to address some issues he was experiencing with his throat. Unfortunately, during this procedure, his doctor erroneously perforated his lungs. After placing him in the intensive care unit, the hospital staff members were able to stabilize him. Eventually, he gained consciousness, but it became challenging for him to speak. As a result, he could only communicate by writing on paper. During this time, I followed my mother's lead and did not worry too much about his condition because we served a God that healed. As a Christian family, we had witnessed God's power. So, it was only fitting that God would heal his servant, a man who had led thousands to Christ, right? No worries! We brushed it off as a minor setback and were confident he would improve in a few days. Unbeknownst to me, Father's Day would be the last time I would see my father alive.

It was a cloudy Friday morning a few days later when my mom received a call from the hospital stating that my father had taken a turn for the worse. My brother rushed to the hospital, summoned everyone out of my father's room, and started praying and petitioning God for my father's life. He would later tell us that was the moment he heard a small voice say, "He is not getting up." Just like that, my father was gone. My brother rushed home in disbelief to tell my mother. But, as he opened the door, he heard the same scream that pierced my soul. Someone had already called her to give her their condolences.

I was fourteen years old, and at that moment, my soul descended into a place of disbelief and fear. I had never imagined that my father could die. I thought that people only died when they got old. With a shattered heart, I began visualizing everything I'd done with my dad. Never having seen any of my friends without a dad, it seemed impossible to me to live my life without one. I felt abandoned. That dark day was the first and last time I witnessed or heard my mother cry. Her scream would echo in my head for months. I remember being told not to cry in front of my mother: "Be strong, Freddie." On that day, I learned how to internalize my pain and put a smile on it.

Because of my father's popularity as a preacher, the news of his untimely death traveled around the world quickly. Not only did his death leave my family devastated, but it also left many Christian believers and his church debilitated and confused. As a result, everyone called my house and came there for comfort. We all mourned together. The day my dad

Daddy preaching

died was the day when I was supposed to graduate from the ninth grade. I was a member of the first graduation class of the Christ Crusader Academy, the school my father had founded. The school officials canceled graduation and replaced it with a day of mourning.

Dad's funeral traumatized me and confirmed the unthinkable: that he would no longer be present in my life. His untimely death left my family shattered and with diminished faith, though we continued to believe that God would take us through. Although available, counseling was not an option for us, an African American Christian family. Trusting in God to handle all our concerns was how we functioned. Additionally, African Americans did not readily seek mental health therapy due to feelings of disconnectedness from the counseling process, trust issues, social stigma, and the desire to keep issues within the family. As a result of not receiving any counseling, we silently suffered, each in a unique way. I suppressed my father's death, relegating it to a place where it could not haunt me.

Even though my mother remained on her knees, praying for strength, wisdom, and guidance, she became a different woman. She was in survival mode and had no road map for surviving without her husband. She now faced the stigma of being vulnerable, lonely, and weak. Beneath the surface surged a deep depression. As a result, she avoided being emotionally transparent and silently mourned for the remainder of her life.

After my father died, my identity changed. As an immature, fourteen-year-old Christian, I felt like God had let me down. As a result, I began viewing love as unbearable, untrustworthy, and unfair. Feeling abandoned, I erected an emotional barrier that prevented me from showing my emotions. I copied my mother's survival skills. I would later learn that I was mimicking a generational and social pattern of women showing up unscathed despite enduring so much.

Studies show that, in the absence of proper mental care when dealing with trauma, one can resort to narrow interpretations of despair. For example, at a youthful age, I created a scenario where I would not let anybody know when I was frightened and sad. Dad's presence was no longer felt around the house. He had always made us second-guess whether we wanted to misbehave. He had confronted our problems head-on, exposed them, and used our issues to help many of his church members overcome theirs. He had never been ashamed of my siblings and me for the choices we had made in life.

Still having my mother in my life helped me tremendously. Her presence softened the anguish of losing my dad and provided some comfort. Although my immature mind was surprised that she was still friends with God, watching her pray and make compelling requests to meet our needs was phenomenal. I did not see how praying and quoting Scriptures would help. However, witnessing God provide for us with resources not present in our lives gave me hope.

Time passed, and the day my dad died disappeared like a passing Eurostar train. Afterward, I began questioning God about many things as I sorted out my feelings.

What's your story?

My father's sudden death caused me to internalize my pain and put a smile on it.

1. What grief has shown up in your life? How have you been able to find moments of joy or happiness amid your grief?

_____

_____

_____

_____

_____

_____

_____

_____

_____

_____

_____

_____

2. Have you observed or created any traditions to honor your loved one's memory or to help you heal?

_____

_____

_____

_____

_____

_____

_____

_____

_____

_____

_____

_____

_____

_____

3

Wolf In Sheep's Clothing

After my father's death sucker punched me in the gut, I assumed a costume of bravery and maturity. Lacking the bandwidth to package my pain correctly, I began immersing myself in activities that absorbed the punches of abandonment and fear. Continuing to run track helped me keep my mind occupied. In track and field, I began to establish an empowering presence. At the same time, track and field was a dark container in which a sexual predator resided.

Now that my dad was no longer in the picture, my track coach began to assume the role of a concerned father. Having the ability to fill in the missing emotional pieces for me, he enabled me to develop an allegiance, enhanced by gratitude and admiration for him.

One afternoon, a few months after my father's passing, interchanging cloudy skies and leaves aggressively falling from trees set the stage for a life-altering day. As I finished up track practice and hastened to change back into my school uniform, my coach offered me a ride. I leaped at the opportunity because I wanted to catch a ride home with my brother and avoid the two-hour journey on the iron horse to Queens. Waving goodbye to my teammates and indicating to some of them to call me later, I jumped into my coach's raggedy station wagon. As we began heading down Lenox Avenue in Harlem toward my destination, my coach praised me for my accomplishments in track. Receiving a dose of affirmation at that moment was like medication, as I was still silently mourning my dad's death.

As we neared my destination, my coach stopped at the corner of Eighth Avenue and 124th Street and parked his car. In my mind, I was thinking, "Why is he stopping? I'm trying to catch a ride home with my brother." Assuming he wanted me to walk the rest of the way, I grabbed my bag. He stopped me and, like a magician, changed into an aggressor that I had never met. It happened so fast. With his right forearm, he pinned me to the seat, forcefully ripped my school tights, and violently shoved his fingers inside me. With my legs stiff like poles, I became motionless, and my tears flowed.

In the broad daylight and with nobody around, he continued to assault me. I lacked the bandwidth to comprehend what was happening. My admiration and respect for him neutralized my thoughts of fighting him off. As he murmured words beyond my comprehension, I yanked open the door and limped out of the car. A different fourteen-year-old girl emerged. As I trudged down the block, wounded, my shame evolved. When I reached my brother's van, I regained my composure, got in, and began chatting with the other kids as if nothing had happened.

At that moment, I was more concerned with covering up the traces of being sexually molested than with my well-being.

Clips of my being sexually molested played in my mind constantly. Day after day, as I contemplated whether I should reveal the trauma I had experienced to my mother, the drumbeats of my heart would play, and tears would dance down my face. Imagining the consequences of my confession, I engaged in one-way conversations with myself daily. Wondering if my coach would be sent to jail, if I could continue running track, and if everyone would blame me rendered me torpid and unable to articulate what had occurred. Moreover, track was the only activity that provided me with structure and mental stability during the period after my father's death. I needed track; it was my therapy, my psych ward. So, I kept quiet.

Not long after I was molested, my mother revealed that her breast cancer had returned. "Cancer!" I yelled. As I was so young, my mother had never told me about the first time she had been diagnosed. Insomnia greeted me for many nights as my mind flooded with thoughts of her dying. I was overwhelmed with sadness thinking about how I would exist if my mother, like Daddy, left me forever. At that time, I believed that disclosing my abuse to my mother would kill her sooner rather than later. What I didn't know at the time was that the day when I vowed not to tell my mother the truth was the day I became the predator's ideal prey. An overwhelming responsibility for keeping my abuse secret consumed me. I became unhinged, fearful, and embarrassed and carried and nursed the shame my abuser should have owned.

I was groomed for the next eight years and developed a bond with my abuser and trauma in order to survive. I subconsciously associated caring with abuse. The abuse would occur at motels, at his job, in his car, and even at his home. Oftentimes, after the assault, he would take me home, speak to my mother, offer his assistance with her personal concerns, then go home to his family.

Given the long days I was putting in for track, there were nights when I would be taken back to crash at his house. I vividly remember that one night, I heard the thumps of his bare feet walking toward the back of his apartment to the room where I slept with his sons scattered like toys on gym mats. My coach crept in and scanned the room like a security guard checking his post. Feeling his presence, I became frightened. My heart began to sprint. As he approached me, I became robotic and adopted a coma-like state, pretending to be asleep. I failed to change his course of action, as he dropped to the floor and began to have sex with me.

"Daddy, Daddy," his son moaned. He paused. His son felt his presence. "It's okay; go back to sleep," he replied while rubbing his son on his back and soothing him back to sleep. I wondered if his son was pretending to be asleep like I was. Did he awaken because he subconsciously knew that what his dad was doing was wrong?

"It's over," I whispered to myself as he wiped any evidence of the crime he had just committed. I sighed as relief consumed me when he left the room.

As the water began pounding into the sink in the next room, I started replaying the orchestrated assault that had just occurred. I was conflicted when pleasure presented itself and my body betrayed me. I thought that its feeling good meant I had complied with the abuse. I quickly tensed up as my coach's silhouette passed across the bedroom door when he walked back toward the living room where he and his wife slept on the sofa bed.

This was what occurred on most nights when I stayed overnight at his house. I was a confused fifteen-year-old girl whose track coach was sexually abusing her. Being abashed kept me quiet because I did not want to get caught in the act of being abused. Moreover, this unhealthy, criminal environment seemed to go some way toward meeting my need for the father who had disappeared from my life upon his untimely death.

The abuse continued, and my abuser started pushing further boundaries sexually. Because his actions were non-violent—which is to say, he did not hit, kick, or slap me—the abuse mimicked the approach of a coach teaching an athlete how to perform.

Sweet 15

When he coached me during track practice, he trained me to become stronger and faster, and when he sexually abused me, he taught me how to be intimate with a man and how to please him.

Mary Ellen Copeland states in her book, *Healing the Trauma of Abuse,* "The ability to choose and define one's physical boundaries is a natural process we learn growing up. However, the process of learning and choosing your physical boundaries can be interrupted or stopped if they are repeatedly violated. This loss can result in repeated abuse, trauma, and victimization."[2]

Copeland's words now resonate so much with me, as being groomed from the time I was a fourteen-year-old child until I was a twenty-two-year-old woman destroyed my capacity to protect my physical boundaries. The grooming process was like kryptonite to my persona and weakened my defenses. However, once I exposed the abuse and was empowered to have agency over my body, I set those boundaries with authority.

What's your story?

Being abused when I lost my father and watching my mother slowly lose her battle to cancer made me appear to be an ideal victim for a predator. The overwhelming responsibility for keeping my abuse secret consumed me. I became unhinged, fearful, and embarrassed and carried and nursed the shame my abuser should have owned.

1. Write about a time when you felt silenced. What caused you to feel that way? How did it impact you?

---

2. What can you do to break through that silence if you have
    not done so?

_____

_____

_____

_____

_____

_____

_____

_____

_____

_____

_____

_____

_____

_____

4

Superwoman

In subsequent years, my stamina and my accomplishments were the loudest indicators of my being superwoman-like. The opportunity to excel in track and field and rise to become one of the nation's top junior athletes provided a platform for me to hide my true identity. In track and field, I was idolized, and I was often a role model to many. Newspaper articles, TV interviews, and all the accolades served as tools to create the image of a powerful, happy girl. As a result, it was easy for me to show up and meet the expectations of everyone, despite what I was secretly enduring. Unfortunately, I was trying to survive a life full of trauma.

Freddie hurdling

The people we visualize as being successful may be living in turmoil that they have hidden from us. Many individuals, such as athletes and actors, who are admired or praised do not have the space to show they are imperfect. Being placed on platforms that make them seem invincible leaves them feeling challenged. They feel pressured to adopt fantasy roles for their admirers. This task keeps them trapped in a world of silent chaos.

Acting like a superwoman gave me this false identity that indicated I could handle whatever came my way. Looking back, because I was taken advantage of at a young age, I wanted to appear strong. It helped hide my true feelings of being afraid, unsure, and lonely. Additionally, within the track arena, I was admired, empowered, awarded; all the girls wanted to be like me. The superwoman persona kept me emotionally imprisoned because I suppressed my emotions for so long, trying to live up to everyone's expectations of me.

Being in the ring with my mother battling cancer while I was being sexually abused months after the unexpected death of my father was one for the books. It felt more important than ever to keep a solid, superwoman persona as things continued to crumble around me.

I was not the only one whose life was turned upside down. Momma was performing and acting like she was okay with her hair falling out from receiving chemo. Witnessing and experiencing what my mother endured during the last four years of her life made me realize one couldn't judge a book by its cover.

My mother always made her situation seem like it was not a big deal until she could not hide it any longer. I mimicked her adaptation skills. At that point in my life, I began to unconsciously adopt the coping mechanism of betrayal blindness. Dr. Jennifer Freyd defines betrayal blindness as not allowing yourself to see what is going on, to connect the dots, or to engage with reality fully because, if you did, the information would threaten your relationship with the person most important to you. Her research states, "Whatever the threatening information may be, we can't let ourselves know about it because it would create such chaos, terror, pain, and confusion that we feel we might not survive it emotionally and psychologically."[3]

My betrayal blindness knew no bounds and was continuously put to the test. Family gatherings at my house during the holidays were like a magical, savory wonderland, and my mother made sure that nothing changed about this, even when she was sick. We loved this time of year because we could see each other and catch up on each other's lives.

My being the youngest of sixteen children meant that some of my older siblings were out of the house, married, or living on their own. My mother always had a special way of making each of us all feel like we were her only child through her unconditional love and support.

In happier days, the house would bustle with children running in and out, my daddy and brothers would be glued to the television watching sports, and my mother would single-handedly cook about fifteen dishes to perfection like a top chef. "Time to eat," was all she had to say to have everyone come simultaneously to the dinner table, forks ready.

Sitting at the table made me feel like a little princess in a royal family, with my daddy being the king and my momma the queen. Gold-trimmed glasses filled with cherry Kool-Aid and dinnerware were positioned perfectly in front of each chair, with sterling silver forks and knives on top of cloth napkins beside the plates. Ceramic dishes of macaroni and cheese, collard greens with smoked ham, and sautéed string beans surrounded a golden forty-pound turkey with homemade stuffing. Sweet potatoes decorated with cotton-sized marshmallows, black-eyed peas and white rice, mashed potatoes whipped to perfection, baked chicken, golden fried chicken, and a ham covered in circular pineapple slices with red cherries pierced through their centers were also on the menu. My mother's favorite sock-it-to-me pound cake; chocolate cake; sweet potato, apple, and peach cobbler pies; and vanilla ice cream were all presented as desserts. Coming together to eat Momma's food always brought us feelings of warmth and happiness.

On Christmas Day of 1981, everything would change. That year, my brother Michael did not show up for dinner. Michael was the seventh oldest child and stood six feet, three inches tall. When he entered a room, he displayed masculine and feminine qualities, simultaneously creating a gender presence outside of either pole. Even though I did not see Michael much, he taught me everything I knew about fashion and ensured I looked and dressed my best when I was in his presence. The house was always lively when Michael was around. His absence from that holiday was concerning, as we didn't hear from him and could not reach him; however, none of us imagined the worst.

We would find out months later the reason Michael did not show up that Christmas Day. Tragically he was a victim of a homicide. His twenty-one-year-old roommate, David Bullock, went on a murdering spree, killing six people, including Michael. This story unfolded in *The New York Times*. As he had been shot in the head and dumped in the frigid East River in Harlem, the recovery of Michael's body took months. His dental records and skeletal features helped the coroner to identify him. Eventually, my brother's murderer, David Bullock, was sentenced to twenty-five years to life for each victim he killed.[4]

Once again, I added a link to my Superwoman armor.

What's your story?

The myth of the superwoman is the furthest from the truth. Her hidden qualities include being docile, afraid, and concerned, constantly worried about whether she will complete the task at hand. She cries and wants help, to be loved, and to be considered. Unfortunately, to protect her vulnerability, she won't ask for help.

1. Do you show up like someone who is mentally strong and has it all figured out but could use a helping hand? Why do you show up this way?

_____

_____

_____

_____

_____

_____

_____

_____

_____

2. What action(s) can you take to become more open to receiving help and support when you need them?

_____

_____

_____

_____

_____

_____

_____

_____

_____

_____

_____

_____

_____

5

Life Is A Whirlwind

Life felt like a whirlwind to me, but through God's help, I held on. Having been exposed to grief lessened the enervating feeling of losing my brother.

Adopting the superwoman persona was a blessing and a curse at the same time. It was a blessing because it kept me fighting to get through what I was enduring but a curse because it allowed me to suppress my true feelings and delay my healing.

A few years had passed since my coach had started sexually abusing me. It had become a routine. He had started introducing me to various birth control methods. This introduction to birth control did not occur in a gynecologist's office with my mother but in a hotel room with my predator. At sixteen years of age, I had a tall athletic build and was still developing into a young lady. Occasionally, I would miss my period for months, and my coach would go into full panic mode. One day, I confided in him (not my mother) that my period was late.

He took me to a clinic where he typically took his clients who lived in a group home setting. He gave me a fake name, and we pretended that I was one of the girls from the system and he was the counselor. He asked them to give me a pregnancy test.

I was a nervous wreck because I knew he would be the child's father if I were pregnant. I was not thinking about how my life would change but about how *his* life would change. Well, thank God the test came back negative. The doctor's diagnosis was that girls my age had irregular periods and I should not worry. While I was in the doctor's examination room, I heard a still, small voice urging me to tell the doctor that I was being sexually abused and didn't know how to make it stop. I struggled and began shaking but could not utter the words. The grooming that victims endure from their abusers keeps them loyal. I kept silent; once again, I was frightened of setting myself free. My silent suffering was now wreaking havoc on my body.

My mother, the backbone of our family, was our greatest advocate no matter what road we chose to travel. As children, we did not make her role easy. Yet she stayed on her knees, requesting God to protect and save us from the evils of this sinful world.

Mommy

As the shifts in my life continued, I would learn that my mother's faith in God as a healer had previously persuaded her to forgo chemotherapy and having her affected breast removed. Being tasked with cleaning her cancerous wounds, which turned into open pus-filled cysts, challenged my belief that God was a healer. Looking upward, I would ask God, "Why is your good and faithful servant going through so much?"

I always tried to encourage my mom by saying her wounds were looking better each day. However, when things got bad for her, she would softly say, "God take me down slowly and bring me up easy."

I read countless stories in the Bible about God's healing, so I'm confident my mother qualified as a beneficiary of His grace. I did not know that my mother was conceding the fight to live and beginning to give me tasks for a future in which she would not be in my life. The deaths of her husband, and son were taking a toll on her. Her health declined rapidly, so she was admitted to Sloan Kettering Hospital to manage her pain. I was unaware that most cancer patients admitted into Sloan Kettering Hospital were in the final stages of their lives and often did not come out alive.

My senior year of high school consisted of attending school, running track, and visiting my mother at Sloan Kettering. When I visited her, I would transform the windowsill in her room into a showcase displaying all the trophies I had won running track. She was always elated, and it gave her a reprieve from the daily chaos in the hospital.

One day, I fell asleep in my mother's hospital bed and was awakened by a loud voice yelling, "Code red!" over the speaker. Many members of staff started running towards a room next to my mother's. They rushed to assist a patient who had stopped breathing, but she did not survive. I went back to sleep, emotionally unfazed by what had just occurred. Experiencing death had become my norm.

In an attempt to spare me from thinking about my mother's dying, no one disclosed the intricate details of her cancer to me. I had not known that she would leave us in months. I had thought she would be coming home. As time had passed, my grandmother had died, along with another brother, leaving me even more emotionally raw.

Some of the nation's top colleges recruited me. Many of them extended invitations to visit their schools with hopes of convincing my mom and me that they were the best fit for me. My momma would read all the recruitment letters with me but did not quite understand the recruiting process. She was just ecstatic about all the offers I was receiving to attend college. I narrowed my choices down to three: the University of Tennessee, Louisiana State University, and the University of Florida. I decided to attend the University of Tennessee, confident that Coach Crawford had the ability and knowledge to train me to be one of the country's best heptathletes.

Soon after, my mother died from cancer. Her passing was bitter-sweet. Of course, I missed her tenacity, courage, affection, and motherly care, but knowing that she no longer had to suffer massaged my heart. Her last four years of battling cancer had taught me about strength and resilience. My mother's favorite Scripture reads, *"Trust in the Lord with all thine heart; and lean not unto thy own understanding. In all thy ways acknowledge him, and he shall direct thy paths"* (Proverbs 3:5–6 KJV).

My mother had trusted in the Lord when her husband had died and when her son had been murdered and dumped in the East River. She had even trusted in the Lord when she had been diagnosed with breast cancer.

While it was heart-breaking, my mother's death was not as emotionally draining as my father's; I had the gift of time to prepare for hers. She died without knowing that someone she trusted was sexually abusing her baby girl. She probably found comfort in death, knowing that my coach was looking after me. Instead, I was now totally vulnerable and dependent on my abuser for emotional support. Once again, I did not receive any counseling. Instead, I struggled and tried to survive without my mother. Her loss dissolved the adhesion that bonded my siblings and me together. As had been the case when my father had died, we all silently suffered her passing in unique ways.

The four years of trauma I endured with the loss of my father, two brothers, grandmother, and mom while being sexually abused became the emotional baggage I carried for many years.

At the time, I had no tools available to me to help me process or understand all I had truly lost. My life kept moving, and it felt like I was just along for the ride.

What's your story?

We've all heard of the expression "make lemonade out of lemons." Life has a way of taking us through challenging times. No matter what trauma you have experienced, you can strengthen that which remains.

1. What steps can you take to prioritize self-care and self-compassion during challenging times?

_____

_____

_____

_____

_____

_____

_____

_____

_____

_____

_____

_____

2. What are some healthy ways for you to process and express emotions related to the trauma you have experienced?

_____

_____

_____

_____

_____

_____

_____

_____

_____

_____

_____

_____

_____

_____

Tennessee Lady Vol

In 1984, being invited to compete in the USA Junior Nationals track meet in Los Angeles, California had me hyped. If I finished in one of the top three places, I would be selected to represent the USA internationally and compete with other juniors around the world. Unfortunately, that track meet occurred the day after my mother's funeral. Despite my emotional condition, my coach, my family, and I decided I should still go to the track meet.

The meet at the Olympic stadium made me feel like I was running to make the Olympic team. It was the most significant arena I had competed in. Even though I appeared excited, I was drowning emotionally. As I was one of the favorites to run well and make the team, many college coaches came to see me compete. Unbeknownst to them, I had already committed and accepted a full athletic scholarship to the University of Tennessee. Chatter was going around at the track meet that Tennessee's coach had taken a head coach position at the University of Texas. My looking forward to being coached by her had me dismissing the rumors. She was a significant factor in my choosing to attend Tennessee.

On the biggest day of my track and field career, I was ready to compete physically, but I could not pull myself together emotionally. As a result, I failed to make the 1984 USA Junior National Team. All I kept thinking about was the fact that my momma was no longer living. I struggled with the reality that I would never see her again.

I went off to college, where I was isolated from my herd of a family and started my new life. With all my trauma packed up in my emotional suitcase, I walked through adversity, conquering my fears and determined to pursue my dreams. The blessing of a full athletic scholarship came at the best possible time. I shifted from being grateful to be the recipient of a scholarship to adhering unwaveringly to maintaining it. I had yet to totally surrender my trauma to God to handle it.

Beginning my journey as a student athlete at the University of Tennessee in Knoxville, Tennessee was hectic. The rumors I'd heard at the USA Junior Nationals turned out to be true: The coach who had recruited me left and took on a new position as head track coach at the University of Texas. As a result, two new coaches assumed the coaching roles for the University of Tennessee women's track and field team. It was like an arranged marriage. I had to establish a relationship with two individuals I did not know. Getting to know one of the new coaches, a Black female, required considerable effort. I surmised that, being only eight years my senior, she lacked the knowledge to coach me.

In addition, my hidden trauma probably made it challenging for her to coach me. Despite the hiccups with the new coaches, I was still ecstatic.

Being a student athlete limited my exposure to many collegiate activities. I was placed on a tight schedule to make sure I remained eligible to compete. My daily routine consisted of going to classes, practice, and study hall. During the weekends, I spent most of my time traveling on a bus or plane from state to state to participate in various track meets. To fit partying with other Black students at the local college into my schedule, I had to do it meticulously. However, being known as a Lady Vol, establishing new relationships, competing, and being treated somewhat like an important person empowered me to embrace this unique experience. "Lady Vol" is a name that the University of Tennessee, Knoxville, adopted to identify the members of its female athletic teams. It arose because the state of Tennessee had become a volunteer state when a large number of volunteers had fought in the war of 1812.[5]

Tennessee Lady Vols

Identifying as a scholar athlete had its benefits. I received free education, room, board, and athletic and academic support. I was recruited along with some of the nation's top athletes and formed fantastic friendships with these ladies. Lavonna Martin-Floréal was one of the girls recruited with me. She and I had known each other as little girls on the Amateur Athletic Union track circuit. Even though we had been competitors, we had admired each other, and now we were teammates at the University of Tennessee (UT). Lavonna would go on to become a two-time Olympian and 1992 silver medalist.

Attending college at UT provided me with an escape from the routine sexual assaults I had endured for the previous four years. I felt that I was finally in a space where I could emerge differently and enjoy being a teenager. I no longer had to conduct myself as though I was a mature young woman. Instead, I was flying like a bird released from its cage, liberated from the constraints of unhappiness.

Even though the abuse stopped for a short period, my abuser stayed in touch with me. As a result of my having no parents, he was my biggest supporter while I was in college. He would even visit under the guise of inquiring about how school and track were going. Like a caring parent, he would send my teammates and me care packages. Thus, I continued falling prey to his emotional tactics. Everyone acknowledged him as a concerned, caring coach. My teammates' acknowledgements persuaded me to stay silent about my trauma.

"Am I the only one being abused?" echoed through my frontal lobe frequently. Unfortunately, it is common for coaches to sexually abuse their athletes. As a matter of fact, the U.S. Center for SafeSport was set up in 2017 under the auspices of the Protecting Young Victims from Sexual Abuse and Safe Sport Authorization Act of 2017. "SafeSport seeks to address the problem of the sexual abuse of minors and amateur athletes in sports. Its primary focus, over which it has exclusive jurisdiction, is reviewing allegations of misconduct and imposing sanctions up to the lifetime banning of a person from involvement in all Olympic sports. One function of SafeSport is to collate a central database of disciplinary cases across all sporting disciplines."[6] Sadly, my situation was not unique.

The outcome of not dealing with my trauma reared its ugly head twice during my college years. Severe abdominal pain and high fevers put me in the hospital at the beginning and end of my college career. An unknown infection kept me hospitalized for over two weeks. Test after test failed to provide any conclusive diagnosis. While in my hospital room, in complete darkness, I did not want anybody visiting me. However, my college coach would come and sit in my room, not knowing that what I was dealing with was far worse than fevers and stomach aches.

I later learned that my failure to thoroughly grieve the deaths of my family members and my absorbing the effects of being sexually abused caused my body to react to the traumas that I had experienced. I was in a constant state of distress but did not know how to release it. Many people are unwell due to not having addressed their traumas. The body always keeps score.

The devil was persistent in destroying my life, but God touched my body and, eventually, I recovered. It wasn't long until I was back to living the life of a student athlete. After enduring a fifty-minute class of solving problems based on slope and speed, I would be found hustling across campus to meet up with my throw coach for practice. I didn't have the time to sunbathe on the lawns of the college campus or play flag football with friends like the other college students did. Track and field were my priority.

I was well into the spring semester of my sophomore year when my life shifted in a new direction. Being a heptathlete required me to master and perform well in seven events. The 100-meter hurdles, long jump, high jump, shot put, javelin, 200-meter run, and 800-meter run were the events I competed in over two days. My training involved a lot of strength work, throwing, speed and hurdle drills, distance running, and track intervals. Practice was often challenging, and juggling school and track had a way of stressing the body.

One hot spring day, my throw coach and I were practicing some javelin throws. Javelin throwing is a highly technical event that requires the perfect coordination of multiple joints in different planes of motion. It involves a run-up of six to ten steps, followed by two or three crossover steps before the thrower releases a spear that is eight feet, two inches long. In the final delivery step, I was transferring the momentum I'd built from the run-up into the javelin when something went awry, and severe pain ripped through my knee.

"Ahh!" I yelled in agony, dropping down on the track and grabbing my leg.

The coach and trainer sprinted over to me just in time to witness my knee swell up to the size of a cantaloupe. As the tears ran down my cheeks, they wrapped my knee with ice, put me on a stretcher, and carried me into the training room. A closer examination resulted in my being transported to the hospital for x-rays. After I received the news that I had torn the meniscus in my right knee and would probably be out for the remainder of the track season, fear and panic set in. The option of having arthroscopic surgery was presented to me as the best method of repairing the tear in my knee. I was not excited, but I felt I had to go through with the surgery because I did not want to jeopardize my scholarship. I had no other financial means in place if I lost my scholarship; my parents were dead.

The surgery was relatively quick and had no complications. As a result of it, I was redshirted, which meant that I did not compete during the period of recovery from my injuries. My track eligibility was extended for the time that I missed because of my injury, which was most of the season. My life after surgery was filled with depressive moments of despair. Just a month before my surgery, I had been walking, running, and jumping. I now had to walk around with crutches, which frustrated me and reminded me of my handicap. Maintaining my motivation to endure painful physical therapy daily drained me mentally, as my everyday tasks were severely altered. It was challenging to sleep, shower, sit down, stand, walk—you name it. My dreams of becoming an Olympian were slowly fading away. I went through the next few weeks feeling sorry for myself.

Alone in my room, sitting at my desk with my injured leg stretched out, I silently whispered, "Why me?" Unable to answer that question, I felt defeat erupting within me. I was frustrated with trying to figure out a way to motivate myself around emotional pit stops once more. Getting to class, sitting in class, getting on elevators, and obtaining my food without requiring assistance were all overwhelming. To be honest, I just wanted to be healed and stress-free without putting in the work to get me to that place of comfort.

After watching students outside my window playing frisbee and sunbathing for weeks, I decided enough was enough. Instead of drowning in the fact that I was injured, I began reminding myself how fortunate I was to be able to rehabilitate my leg and maintain my scholarship. I started to eliminate the negative thoughts and to believe that I could endure and persevere. God was beginning to do a new thing with me. Getting off my crutches was my top priority, and achieving that goal came with a lot of effort and tears. When the spring semester ended, I went home for the summer and continued to heal. Thinking back, I always felt that I never reached my full athletic potential. Throughout the remainder of my college career, I silently struggled with my emotions *and* athletics.

What's your story?

The outcome of not dealing with my trauma reared its ugly head twice during my college years. Severe abdominal pain and high fevers put me in hospital at the beginning and end of my college career.

1. What are some coping strategies you used in the past that helped you manage your health in times of stress?

_____

_____

_____

_____

_____

_____

_____

_____

_____

_____

_____

2. Have you sought professional help or support? If not, what barriers
   have prevented you from doing so?

_____

_____

_____

_____

_____

_____

_____

_____

_____

_____

_____

_____

_____

_____

3. What steps can you take to prioritize your health and self-care during a difficult time?

_____

_____

_____

_____

_____

_____

_____

_____

_____

_____

_____

_____

_____

4. Are there any triggers or reminders that worsen your symptoms? How can you minimize exposure to them?

_____

_____

_____

_____

_____

_____

_____

_____

_____

_____

_____

_____

_____

_____

_____

7

The Big Apple

The house I grew up in as a child was located in the Big Apple. After my mother died, my sister, Gloria, moved in and took full responsibility for its upkeep. The home I'd known had changed. The household I'd grown up in, with many relatives coming in and out of the revolving front door and grabbing a bite of Momma's cooking, no longer existed. Momma's death had affected everyone. After a while, everyone stopped showing up, and the next time most of us got together again, it was for a Thanksgiving dinner many years later.

Traveling back home during the summer months gave me a reprieve, enabling me to indulge in what I'd not been able to do at school. Tennessee was dull compared to the hustle and bustle of New York City. Hopping on and off trains, running to the park to play handball, and shopping in the popular places on Jamaica Avenue and in Albee Square Mall to grab the latest finds was exciting. It wasn't long before my coach caught up with me and began abusing me again. His favorite place to take me was a motel in the Parkchester section of the Bronx.

He would take me there so often that I made a game of trying to guess which room we would go into. Every time we went there, I numbed myself to what was occurring. I did what I had to do to finish as quickly as possible.

I remember one night when the hotel was bustling; people were coming in and out nonstop. As I sat in the car, waiting for my abuser to return with the keys, I locked eyes with the man at the desk. I began asking myself why he was not coming to rescue me from this ordeal. I knew he had to see that I was a child with a grown man. I guess it was all about the money. Eventually, my coach returned to the car with the key, and we quickly ran into the room. The room was not as nice as an actual hotel room. It did not have many lights, smelled stale, and had only one bed.

During this time in my life, I was suffering from Stockholm syndrome. In my research, I have learned that Stockholm syndrome explains how a relationship can form between a victim and their abuser. Although it is a complex psychological response, it is believed to occur when the victim begins to sympathize with the captor. Due to the victim's fear, the emotions that they feel can grow into attachments. It is a condition that can develop in more than one scenario. It's often found in children who have been abused, battered women, cult members, victims of incest, and those involved in controlling relationships. Although it is recognized as a victim's strategy for survival, it can cause the victim to form an emotional bond with the abuser and allow the dangerous activity to continue. In an attempt to survive, the victim might defend or even love the controller. This is dangerous, as the victim can feel positive emotions toward them, support their rationales, and avoid doing anything to gain control.

By the time I was nineteen years old, I thought I would no longer be considered a victim because of my age. I did not realize that my ability to say no and set limits was severely damaged. I viewed every failed test, every race I lost, and every bad experience as my punishment for having sex with my coach. Only later did I learn that his role as an authority figure in my life made him the one responsible. When a victim matures in age, they do not suddenly become a responsible, cooperative partner in sexual abuse. If you are being sexually abused, especially if you have been abused from childhood to adulthood, it's not your fault.

It was a typical summer day when my niece and I decided to go shopping in Brooklyn. Fate was hard at work. Getting off at the wrong stop forced us to ask a stranger for proper directions. That was when my heart somersaulted into the arms of a man who would awaken my ability to love. He introduced himself as Abdel. My niece was so enamored of his African print hat that she asked him where she could purchase one. He said he sold them and handed me a card. His giving me the card was awkward, as my niece had asked for it, but I grabbed it and thanked him, and off we went. Just a few minutes later, we heard Abdel yelling, "Excuse me, excuse me!" Struggling to catch his breath, this stranger poured his soul out about how smitten he was when he saw me. He did not want to let the moment go without getting a way to contact me. I obliged him and handed him my digits.

In the later part of the summer, I enrolled in summer school to gain additional credits as Abdel and I began a verbal love affair. Over the phone, we spent countless hours exposing the conditions of our hearts and revealing our past adversities and triumphs. Having an intimate conversation with a man was different for me. My heart began to feel massaged in a way it never had before. By the beginning of the next school year, we had become the perfect couple, and my mindset began transforming from a prisoner's into a conqueror's.

Abdel, aka Gege, was born in Monrovia, Liberia, and was one of five children. Moving to the United States from Africa at the tender age of two gave him the vibe of being a Black American man. He was raised Catholic but embraced the teachings of Islam while incarcerated and began calling himself Abdel. As a young, immature Christian, I did not know much about Islam, but I knew the associated beliefs contradicted what Christians believed. Our intimate conversations provoked transparent confessions of how he had been falsely accused of sexually assaulting his ex-girlfriend and had been incarcerated as a result. He fell prey to the judicial system, which scared him into taking a plea or risking receiving a sentence of fifteen to twenty years if he went to trial.

He described feeling powerless and vulnerable against a system that viewed all Black men as perpetrators. I cannot explain the peace in my heart that resulted from his confession to having been incarcerated for sexually assaulting a woman. By this time in my life, I had been abused for many years and was still sexually involved with my coach from time to time. You would think I would have run away and avoided dealing with Abdel, but that was not the case. I can't explain why, but I believed him. In my present state, in which I have done some mental health work to heal, I don't know if I would have reacted the same way. Even though my relationship with him was comforting and I began to transform mentally from a prisoner into a conqueror, I did not initially tell him I was being sexually abused. That disclosure would come at another time.

I was still holding tight to my superwoman persona, balancing the outward success in my life with the secrets, pain, and grief I was holding on to behind the scenes.

What's your story?

Stockholm syndrome is a complex psychological response; it is believed to occur when a victim begins to sympathize with their captor.

In an attempt to survive, the victim might defend or even love the controller. This is dangerous as the victim can feel positive emotions toward their abuser, support their rationales, and avoid doing anything to gain control.

1. Have you ever engaged in unhealthy behaviors to cope with difficult situations? Write about those experiences and how you have worked to change those patterns.

---

2. Reflect on a time when you felt overwhelmed by your emotions. What strategies did you use to manage those feelings?

_____

_____

_____

_____

_____

_____

_____

_____

_____

_____

_____

_____

_____

_____

8

Empowered

I made it! I graduated. I felt so accomplished on that day. Even though my family was not present to celebrate the joyous occasion with me, I was happy. My circumstances might have indicated a different scenario, but God was still walking with me. My two college suitemates and my coach and his family were my guests at my graduation. My coach seemed like a proud dad.

When I left Tennessee, I was a completely different person. I did not realize that through my college years, whenever I had felt defeated, I was in the process of becoming spiritually, emotionally, and mentally stronger. Victor Frankel states, "Suffering in and of itself is meaningless: we give our suffering meaning by the way in which we respond to it."[7] I was now ready to talk about the abuse I had endured. I decided to share my story with my brother, Robert. I was so nervous about what I would say and how he would react. Having been abused for several years had left me emotionally invested in my coach. I had felt obligated to keep our secret.

My intentions in telling my brother were not for my coach to get in trouble but for the sexual abuse to cease. I wanted to live a life completely free from him and to love Abdel without any distractions. Speaking up was a significant undertaking in so many ways. Trying to minimize the severity of what had occurred had left me unable to describe what had happened to me thoroughly. My coach's behavior of constantly calling and wanting to see me had become obsessive and overwhelming.

I decided to make Robert a co-owner of my trauma. He was living the life of a disciplined Christian man, preaching, and doing God's work. When my parents died, my brother Robert inherited a lot of responsibilities and was overwhelmed with triaging many of our family's burdens. Because he had already assumed a parental role in my life, I felt he would be the best person to confide in. My other brothers, who already had histories with the criminal system, would possibly have hurt or maybe even considered killing my coach. I would have felt horrible about any such outcome. I had mastered the art of carrying everyone's burden instead of tending to my own. Ultimately, I followed through. On a summer day following my graduation, I called my brother and asked him to stop by after work. He agreed. I waited to exhale the many years of trauma I had endured.

Chimes echoed throughout the house as a dark shadow appeared in front of the door. My brother had arrived. As he walked in, he began complaining about the traffic he had experienced coming from Manhattan to Queens. As we sat on the front porch, my anxiety rose to an uncomfortable level that almost caused me to lose my nerve, but I went for it. Gently, I interjected. As I spoke in detail about the sexual abuse I had endured, he stared with sorrowful eyes, listening attentively. Once I had finished, Robert released a gush of air as his head swayed like a pendulum. He apologized, stating he felt somewhat responsible for not protecting me. Immediately, I felt distressed that he blamed himself.

"It's not your fault!" I yelled.

He mentioned that he'd thought something was off between the coach and me but could not pinpoint specifics without any evidence given the damage that accusations would have caused.

As an aside, parents, if you suspect something wrong is occurring in your child's life, trust your instincts. Investigate by asking your child questions. Often, the abuser is someone that the child and family know well. Yes, things can get complicated if the predator is a family member. Prepare yourself to have to make some tough decisions. Don't sweep any abuse under the rug. Abuse is a vicious, cyclical crime, and often, when victims do not receive proper care, they have to come to their own unhealthy understanding of what happened to them. Lack of help can lead to all kinds of problems.

Earlier in my life, I probably would have denied the abuse was happening if my brother had asked me about it, but with my newfound boldness, I petitioned him to help stop the abuse by talking with my coach. He complied! Like detectives, my brother and I planned to have my coach meet us at a church. Ironically, it was located on the block where he first molested me. His quick acceptance proved that he had no idea he would be confronted about abusing me. Remember, for years, he had successfully groomed me to keep quiet about the abuse. So, why would he suspect that I had told someone?

Even at that life-altering moment, recalling how I had felt when my father had suddenly disappeared from my life persuaded me to tell my brother that I did not want my abuser to go to jail. I was concerned about what would happen to his three little boys' well-being if they no longer had access to him. As we descended into the basement of the church building, the little soldiers began to dance in my heart.

Like the preacher he was, my brother focused all his attention on Coach B. He began to recite everything I had confided in him about what the coach had done to me. Coach B looked down in the middle of the speech to avoid locking eyes with my brother. My brother paused as he waited for a response. Finally, my coach looked up and said, "No, I didn't." Like a true predator, he denied he ever had sex with me.

With my newfound spirit of boldness maturing, I screamed at him with wide eyes, "Yes, you did." I then went into an all-out verbal rage, vomiting up the most heinous crimes he'd committed against me and when and where they had taken place. When I stopped screaming, I was panting as though I had run the 100-yard dash. Robert grabbed my hand to comfort me and, slowly and in a deep pitch, said directly to my coach, "I am trying to deal with you as a man of God and not as her brother. Please do not make this outcome unpleasant."

Displaying a look of defeat, Coach B stated he would stop. I felt free at that moment. It was as if an enormous object had been taken off my back. I walked out of that church like a freed prisoner. The consequences I had associated with breaking my silence had been false. From that day on, the relationship between my coach and me shifted in that he stopped acting like a predator. We moved forward as if nothing had ever happened between us.

The modification in his behavior sanctioned me to live in forgiveness of him. My kind act of forgiveness granted me the freedom to have healthy relationships, to not be tormented by my having been abused, and to not become dependent on drugs or alcohol as my idols of comfort. Unfortunately, what I identified as moving forward back then was inaccurate. There was still a lot of work to do. I didn't know that I should have started therapy at that time. By not addressing what had happened to me, I only suppressed my trauma. It would lie dormant until I faced it again. Culturally, suppressing trauma and acting as if nothing has occurred are the actions many families choose. My mother did it, and I was now repeating a generational cycle. Unfortunately, this tactic was debilitating and left me feeling insignificant. In some instances, if the abuser is within the family, the victim is forced to simultaneously relive and suppress their trauma at the subconscious level. As a result, I continued moving through life trying to please everyone while in pursuit of my healing.

What's your story?

Victor Frankel states, "Suffering in and of itself is meaningless: we give our suffering meaning by the way in which we respond to it." After enduring a lot, I became spiritually, emotionally, and mentally stronger.

1. What positive changes have you noticed in yourself since enduring a traumatic experience?

_____

_____

_____

_____

_____

_____

_____

_____

_____

_____

_____

2. How can you continue to build on these strengths?

_____

_____

_____

_____

_____

_____

_____

_____

_____

_____

_____

_____

_____

_____

_____

9

Love/Grief

Time marched forward, and soon after, Gege asked me to connect my life with his eternally. Who would have thought that a victim of childhood sexual abuse would accept love, trust love, and embrace love? Something had been murdered in me during my childhood, but it had not been love. Never in a million years had I thought I would be emotionally fit for love. For most of my teenage years, the devil had tried to convince me I didn't matter, but the enemy's lies had been exposed again.

Wedding

Whisking us into a fairy-tale journey, our African-inspired wedding allowed us to fully embrace our cultures while displaying our adoration and intentions for one another. The wedding was beautiful. Gold and metallic pink two-piece outfits with matching head wraps and gold shoes adorned the women. The men wore black and gold pants and dashiki shirts with Kofi hats. All my guests embraced the theme and showed up in their best African-inspired garments.

The reception hall, transformed into a regal African gala, resembled a palace fit for a king and queen, with flowers, African fabric, ornaments, and candles serving as décor. As I walked down the aisle in a fitted custom-made ivory lace dress drizzled with pearls and a head wrap to match, my guests stared. They were wide-eyed with admiration and happiness. My king wore an ivory traditional African three-piece outfit with a matching Kofi hat to complement my gown. We represented African royalty.

Not too long afterward, God honored our commitment and blessed us with a beautiful baby girl. Her birth completed our family unit and cemented our purpose as we honored our roles as parents. My God-inspired marriage served as recompense from God for the ill-fated trauma I had sustained. However, my life would soon shift down the familiar road of grief again.

Hubby and baby

Gege owned a music distribution business, which kept him traveling to and from conferences, trade shows, and festivals. So, when he decided to open two stores in Manhattan, I became more involved and began understanding and embracing the ins and outs of being a business owner. Our main store, located on 125th Street in Harlem, opposite the world-famous Apollo Theater, was our busiest location.

Being surrounded by street vendors and other Black entrepreneurs was empowering for us as young business owners. The hustle and bustle of tourists and neighborhood customers continuously entering and leaving our store helped it to become one of the most popular music stores on 125th Street.

On a particularly busy day, with the sun shining like a spotlight on the Mart, my husband's friend came into the store and uttered words that would change my life: "Sis, I have horrible news; your husband was in a car accident, and he is deceased."

I was confused and asked him to repeat what he had said. My brain couldn't compute his message. The word "deceased" held no meaning.

"Your husband is dead," he repeated.

I started screaming, "Noooooo!" I dropped to the floor, grabbed my friend's legs, and wailed uncontrollably. Then I began feeling nauseous, faint, and hot all at once.

Sadly, during his trip, Gege's car flipped over several times. He had been ejected from his vehicle, breaking his neck and losing his life. Word quickly got around Harlem about my husband's death. Everyone rushed to the store as if we were having a clearance sale. They held their heads, crying, as they surrounded my daughter and me. Even though I had already experienced the loss of my father, mother, three brothers, and grandmother, the pain I experienced when I lost my husband was unbearable. This pain was unfamiliar. I became numb.

The day arrived when I had to view my husband's body. I was extremely nervous, but at the same time, I needed confirmation that he was dead. When I entered the viewing room and laid eyes on my king, he appeared to be sleeping. I began apologizing to him for the way he had died as tears streamed down my face. My family members eventually came in to view his body and were in disbelief when they saw him in a coffin. At that moment, while holding my baby, I realized it was all on me. When my husband died, I was on extended maternity leave, and he was the sole provider. I was a housewife and had been in no rush to return to work.

Six months after giving birth, I was consumed with immense grief. My capacity to perform as a widow and single parent was restricted; I required assistance from family and friends. This unfamiliar journey was painful and showed up uninvited at the happiest time of my life. Being a single parent meant I was solely responsible for providing for my child, but I was emotionally unavailable for the task. I was breastfeeding my baby when my husband died, but because I did not want to eat, get out of bed, or be around anyone, that became too difficult. My family agreed when my nephew, Ali, stated he would stay with me and help me around the house. As I stayed confined to my room, my prison for my daughter and me, he

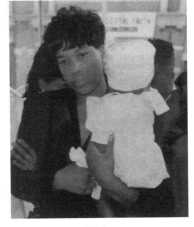

Widow

would sit by my side and make sure I ate by passing me my food and drink. Day by day, God provided me with the strength to continue providing for my baby.

I thought God had given up on me. I truly believed my prayers did not go beyond the ceiling. I would never have imagined that thirteen years after my father's death, I would be experiencing the very same grief my own mother had experienced. I began questioning God: Why was I suffering so much adversity?

"Is this a generational curse?" I pondered. The devil was doing a number on me, trying to convince me to give up. However, Romans 8:28 reminded me, *"All things work together for good to them that love God, to them who are the called according to his purpose"* (KJV).

"All things?" I pondered.

Single parenting had me showing up like a superwoman. I felt it was my responsibility to embrace my new role and suppress my true countenance of sadness. I raised my daughter, providing her with the emotional tools to protect her mind and body. In her life, I became the person I had needed in *my* life as a child: a teacher, a protector and a provider. Unfortunately, I thought that being a responsible parent as she grew up meant that I should not burden her emotionally. As a result, I never let her see me cry.

Whenever I experienced difficulties as a widow or single parent or stress from work or being a homeowner, I would retreat to my basement and weep. I was subconsciously mimicking my family's generational survival tactics. Revealing the cause of my tears would not change my circumstances, so I suppressed my feelings. When you do not allow yourself to express your grief, it festers. Buried grief poisons, affecting how you show up emotionally and, in turn, how you deal with people.

I would later learn from my daughter that I had altered how she expressed her emotions. My showing up emotionless in her life made her feel that something was wrong with her when she became emotional. That superwoman persona was holding her hostage.

What's your story?

The danger with suppression is that it puts one's issues and emotions in an incubator, where they often grow and multiply, becoming more challenging to bear.

1. Write about a time when you felt like you had to suppress your emotions. What prevented you from dealing with your feelings? How did you cope with that situation?

_____

_____

_____

_____

_____

_____

_____

_____

_____

_____

_____

2. Reflect on a time when you felt overwhelmed by your emotions. What strategies did you use to manage those feelings? Why? Did you seek help?

_____

_____

_____

_____

_____

_____

_____

_____

_____

_____

_____

_____

_____

_____

_____

10

Savior

While I was transitioning into my new role as a widow and single parent, my child was my main priority. Yet I had to make real-life decisions that placed me at a crossroads. I needed a more secure job with better pay. The tough decision to pursue a career in law enforcement became my reality. My sister, an active detective, and my niece, a police officer, advised me to take advantage of the opportunity. After being a social worker for eight years, I started my career in law enforcement with the New York City Police Department.

"Attention on deck!" bellowed from the belly of a police sergeant mimicking an army drill sergeant. Half the recruits and I jumped to attention like soldiers, and the other half did so like broken toys, wondering what had just happened. If my sister and niece had not prepared me, I would have been oblivious about what to do on day one of the police academy. As only half of the group moved, the sergeant commanded us, "Front, lean, and rest." The bulk of us dropped down into a push-up position. I silently asked myself, "What have I gotten myself involved in?"

During these challenges, many recruits quit right on the spot. I would learn that weeding out those who displayed physical and mental limitations was the academy's goal during this so-called Hell Week. For the next nine months, I continued to be challenged physically, emotionally, mentally, and even spiritually while in the police academy. The preparation of the recruits determined the type of day I would have. The academy's goal was for us not only to learn New York State's penal laws but to also be challenged and acquire the bandwidth to deal with the demands of being a police officer.

After enduring nine mentally and physically exhausting months of training, I graduated and was chosen to work in the 70th Precinct, located in the southern section of Brooklyn, New York. As a result of a recent heinous crime, my precinct was under siege, and the National Guard was activated for several months to assist us. Months of rioting and civil unrest shaped the atmosphere I worked in daily. *This is not what I signed up for,* I constantly thought. I was a rookie cop who feared for her safety every day. However, great benefits, great pay, and a twenty-year commitment to receive a pension were high motivators that kept me going.

Wearing a blue uniform as a Black female sometimes placed me in the penalty box even though I was not the person responsible for the associated atrocity. The work schedule, the nature of the job, and my role as a single parent and officer were challenging and often in conflict. Society had embraced ideologies that implied that being a Black female meant being inferior, "less than," yet superwoman-like and able to handle anything. These labels were set in place to limit my opportunities in life and to keep me in a position of insignificance.

I always felt that being a female officer came with risks. It was not something I advertised when I was off duty. Early in my career, I detected that my community was against my being a cop. Today, however, I realize their prejudices were a reaction to unfair historical practices directed at people of color. In their eyes, policing was another way of subjecting them to slavery.

Cupid revisited me, and I started dating. It felt awesome to be loved again and to have a companion who genuinely cared for my daughter and me. This relationship was awesome for eight years, but it caused an emotional reset when it ended. I refused to stay where I had begun to feel irrelevant, and my capacity to heal was strengthened.

I continued to identify as a widow, like my mother had thirteen years prior. But I found myself irritated with the term itself. Whenever I had to complete any paperwork and "widow" was one of the relationship status options, I never selected it. I felt more powerful choosing "single."

When an opportunity to become an officer with a different police department became available, I was somewhat apprehensive. Yet, attracted by a greater salary, excellent benefits, and a better working environment, I entered the Port Authority Police Academy. Their academy was like a military boot camp. However, due to my athletic abilities and previous successful stint at the NYPD's academy, I graduated and was sworn in as a police officer. I was initially assigned to the world-famous bus terminal and quickly got into the rhythm of my new command. Located in the heart of New York City's Times Square, my new beat bustled with drug addicts and dealers, runaways, and criminals, creating a chaotic and tumultuous environment. Even though the Port Authority was a private police department, the working conditions at the bus terminal mirrored the demanding conditions I had left.

As had happened at the NYPD, horrible, frightening working conditions emerged. On September 11, 2001, my life changed, along with thousands of others' lives, as NYC became the victim of a terrorist attack by an Islamic extremist group, Al-Qaeda. The terrorists hijacked four commercial planes and deliberately crashed two into the North and South towers of the World Trade Center. "A third plane hit the Pentagon in Arlington, Virginia, and the fourth plane crashed in Shanksville, Pennsylvania, after passengers overcame the terrorists. The attack resulted in the deaths of nearly 2,977 people."[8] Of them, thirty-seven victims were Port Authority cops. For the next two years, assisting with rescue and recovery and working sixteen-hour shifts would be my new norm. Even though this experience was very stressful, I found the strength to manage and juggle my roles as mother and officer to honor the fallen heroes.

I continued to make my presence known within the police department. Eventually, I was selected to work as a police instructor in the police academy. Having the opportunity to meet aspiring officers as rookies allowed me to impact their lives early in their careers. As a sergeant, I would often remind the officers that even though our goal for the day was to protect life and property, we had to put ourselves first. We had to deal with the personal issues hiding beneath our vests and plaguing our lives before we could truly be of assistance. The law enforcement arena often does not provide an atmosphere in which many officers can be vulnerable about their mental states.

They usually find help for their mental health in secret. Seeking help can result in one's being labeled unfit for duty and losing wages.

Navigating through the rest of my career consisted of being prepared to fight crimes, survive injustice, and expect nothing and being prepared for anything. After twenty-two years in law enforcement, overcoming many obstacles and challenges allowed me to retire as a trailblazer in women's policing. I was also instrumental in

Achievements

ARFF Instructor Makes History

PA News was recently informed that Port Authority Police Officer **Frederica Tokponwey** made agency history in January 2016, when she became the first woman officer to serve as an instructor in the Aircraft Rescue and Firefighting training academy.

Officer Tokponwey is a 15-year veteran of the PAPD. Prior to joining the PA, she served as a police officer in the NYPD for close to four years, and helped in the 9/11 recovery efforts.

In addition to her impressive police experience, Officer Tokponwey serves as a life and health coach, and is an active member at the Soul Saving Station Church in Harlem, where her brother, Bishop Robert I. Winley, is the overseer.

achievements

creating several training components that were taught to all ranks within the police department.

In 2016, I was honored to be the first female firefighter instructor in Port Authority history, empowering many officers to go after what seemed impossible.

Sergeant

What's your story?

In my roles as a police sergeant, social worker, and single parent, I had opportunities to positively impact those under my influence. Single parenting had me showing up like a superwoman and caused me to conceal my true countenance of sadness.

1. Can you share any specific strategies or techniques you use to inspire and motivate others?

---

2. Have you ever faced challenges when trying to influence others? If so, how did you overcome them?

_____

_____

_____

_____

_____

_____

_____

_____

_____

_____

_____

_____

_____

_____

3. Have you ever been in a parental role or a role of influence in which the outcome proved different from what you expected?

_____

_____

_____

_____

_____

_____

_____

_____

_____

_____

_____

_____

_____

11

Overcomer

Living my life with trauma and accomplishments in tow, I began to marvel at how God had adored me and carried me through my wilderness. I came to a point in my life where I felt that I needed to uncover some of my childhood traumas because they were part of who I had become. Shame, timing, and not having the wherewithal to communicate were all reasons I had chosen not to speak about my past for many years.

Just when I had been two months shy of turning fourteen, my life had transformed from a stress-free childhood filled with happy expectations and experiences into incomprehensible trauma and tragedies in succession. As I continued praying and began writing and pushing towards the pain in order to heal, I uncovered the inauthentic person I was living through. My historical traumatic events determined how I showed up and dealt with people. I learned that my pain had become my perspective in life.

When I started being transparent about having been sexually abused, people asked what the consequences of my coach's actions had been. I felt wrong when I answered, "Nothing."

I recently had a talk with my brother about the day I made him a co-owner of my secrets. He confessed that, as time passed, he realized he should have handled my situation differently. He stated that he had always intended to address my coach again about what he had done to me and wanted an opportunity to confront him once more. I agreed and told him recently that I was also thinking about confronting him, this time as a mature woman who had lived and survived the trauma of being abused.

This idea came about after I had a conversation with my daughter about my coach's use of contraceptives with me. "That shows intent," she responded, angrily. She was, once again, infuriated at what he had done to me and began to explain how unfair it was that he had not been held accountable for his actions. At that moment, something shifted in me. Suddenly, the little fourteen-year-old girl who could not defend herself emerged in my conscious mind. I wanted to speak up for her.

My brother contacted my coach and asked him for a face-to-face meeting. My coach initially agreed; however, months went by and he never followed through. Not wanting to force a conversation and give him the power to control the outcome, I decided against contacting him again.

If I'd had the opportunity to converse with him, I would have let him know, from a forgiven heart, how his actions had affected and changed my life. On the day when my brother and I had initially confronted him, I had sought to stop the abuse. Unfortunately, from that day forward, I attempted to bury the effects of being sexually abused as if it had never happened. Keeping secrets for years caused me a lot of psychological impairment.

If an opportunity presents itself and you feel you have done the work to confront your accuser, explore what it might mean to do so. Even though I did not have a conversation with my abuser again, this book serves as my testimony of what I endured and overcame. I am not the same wounded girl anymore.

When I was in the height of agony, I began writing, birthing one recollection at a time with all the attached elements. I dug deep to uncover the incidents I had suppressed; they brought about metaphoric labor pains as they were birthed. I identified my traumas as silently living through childhood sexual abuse and the sudden and unanticipated deaths of my parents, siblings, grandmother, and husband. The placenta of shame, depression, loss of trust, abandonment, unworthiness, and anger all came forth through revelations in therapy.

Most people are weakest emotionally in their childhoods. The sudden loss of my dad took me on an emotional expedition, causing my mental collision with confusion, abandonment, and betrayal. My protective covering vanished. The irrefutable cognition that cancer would kill my mother terrified me. As a result of the emotional trauma I endured, I became the ideal victim of a sexual predator.

Like an addict craving emotional repair and yearning to ease the pain of grief, I succumbed to the grooming of my sexual abuser as he methodically broke down my defenses. I know the agony one experiences when dealing with pain is unimaginable. I was able to identify and begin to heal from all of this through my therapeutic experience.

The result of my journey towards healing from all my adversities was that I refused to remain buried in my circumstances. As long as I identified with being a victim, being angry, being depressed, and possessing an unforgiving spirit, my recovery would be slow. When I surrendered and accepted God's gift of forgiveness, I began walking towards healing. Years of impaired thinking began unraveling. The process did not happen quickly, but through it all, I was strengthened mentally, spiritually, and emotionally.

Job 36:15 reads, *"God delivers the afflicted by their afflictions and makes himself known to them by their suffering"* (KJV).

From my healing journey, I have learned that you find the antidote and heal when you do the work. When I speak of doing the work, I mean taking purposeful steps towards self-healing, which is a lifelong commitment. Often, because healing can be difficult and time-consuming, we fight against the work instead of embracing it. Suppressing your feelings and pretending that they are not valid only prolongs your healing. Author, Terrie Williams says, this action causes the suppressed trauma to "come back stronger through another door, asserting itself in the form of alcohol abuse, fear of relationships, panic attacks, hopelessness—and if it goes on long enough, it will turn into depression."[9]

I petition you to ask for help, face your issues, and begin changing your relationship with your trauma. Stop pretending to be a superhero whose emotions have not been compromised by painful experiences. Be kind to yourself.

Ellen Bass said it best in her book, *The Courage to Heal*: After a lifetime of loneliness, it can be challenging to develop close relationships or even trust anyone, which is at the heart of the healing process. Most of us have suffered abuse in silence because of shame, but we don't have to heal in the same lonely isolation. Part of healing involves being around supportive people.[10]

Seeking affirmation from people is outsourcing your faith. You are more than enough and can surpass any obstacle that is placed in your life. Look at what you've lived through so far. Yes, it may mean that you have to endure more challenges or wait longer than you anticipated. However, in the pursuit of healing, you will become more resilient, more strategic, and equipped with more emotional tools to persevere. I believe you can do all things through Christ, so whatever you pursue, desire, and believe will eventually happen for you.

The power of God helped me triumph over my circumstances, and now I use my trauma as a platform to empower others. When I was going through my trauma, I thought I was cursed. Now, I am confident that as God was taking me through, he was perfecting me and preparing me for my purpose. I continue to serve as a conduit of hope by speaking on my podcast, *Debunking the Myth of a Superwoman*, and on different women's empowerment platforms.

I petition you to do the necessary work in your life so that you can be set free from your past. Seek therapy to deal specifically with your emotional issues, surround yourself with like-minded women, and form a sacred space in which to share with and empower one another. God's healing and grace remains available to us all.

It's your Time to Shine!

Empowerment Speaker

What's your story?

With God's help, I began talking about the trauma I had persevered through. That, in turn, empowered many of my listeners to speak up and break free from the emotional prisons that had caused them to live diminutive lives.

1. Use this moment to break your silence and find your voice and begin journaling about what had/has you emotionally stuck.

_____

_____

_____

_____

_____

_____

_____

_____

_____

_____

_____

2. Reflect on a time when you felt empowered and transformed. What techniques did you use to achieve your transformation? Someone needs your story to heal.

_____

_____

_____

_____

_____

_____

_____

_____

_____

_____

_____

_____

_____

My daughter and I

It's your Time to Shine

The following pages are yours to use as you wish. You may choose to dig deeper into your story. You may begin to dream up your own next chapter. You hold the pen. It's your time to shine.

References

1. Bass, Ellen, and Davis Laura. (2008). *The Courage to Heal: A Guide for Women Survivors of Child Sexual Abuse*. Twentieth Anniversary Edition (Fourth Edition). Harper & Row Publishers. p. 33.

2. Ellen, Mary and Harris, Maxine. (2000). *Healing the Trauma of Abuse*. New Harbinger Publications. p. 33.

3. *Jennifer Joy Freyd, PhD*. Jennifer Joy Freyd, PhD. https://www.jjfreyd.com

4. The Associated Press. (1982, Oct 27). Man Pleads Guilty to 6 Murders. *The New York Times*. https://www.nytimes.com/1982/10/27/nyregion/man-pleads-guilty-to-6-murders-says-killing-makes-me-happy.html

5. *The University of Tennessee, Knoxville | UT Timeline*. The University of Tennessee, Knoxville | UT Timeline. https://Timeline.utk.edu

6. United States Center for SafeSport. (2022, November 21). In *Wikipedia*. https://en.wikipedia.org/wiki/United_States_Center_for_SafeSport

7. Frankl, Viktor. (1962). *Man's Search for Meaning*. Beacon Press.

8. *Homepage | National September 11 Memorial & Museum*. Homepage | National September 11 Memorial & Museum. https://911memorial.org/

9. Williams, Terrie Black. (2008). *Pain: It Just Looks Like We're Not Hurting*. Simon & Schuster.

10. Bass, Ellen, and Davis Laura. (2008). *The Courage to Heal: A Guide for Women Survivors of Child Sexual Abuse*. Twentieth Anniversary Edition (Fourth Edition). Harper & Row Publishers. p. 30.

ABOUT THE AUTHOR

Meet Frederica Tokponwey, a passionate motivational speaker, dynamic podcaster, and nurturing mother. She's all about inspiring women to rise about their challenging beginnings. Frederica has been invited to share her wisdom with several women's empowerment forums, and has garnered recognition from esteemed organizations like the National Organization of Black Women in Law Enforcement. She sparks resilience and inspires women to reach their true potential.

Through her empowering podcast, "Debunking the Myth of a Superwoman," Frederica urges her listeners to embrace transparency and let go of the expectation of being a superwoman who juggles everything and neglects their own well-being. Instead, she encourages them to tap into their authentic "superpower" within their hearts and minds.

Facebook: Frederica Tokponwey
IG: iamfredericaa

Website: Fredericatokponwey.com

Email: contact@overcomerunleashed.com

Made in the USA
Middletown, DE
01 April 2024

52290343R00068